WHY BUSINESS THINKING
IS NOT THE ANSWER

GOOD TO GREAT
AND THE
SOCIAL SECTORS

A Monograph to Accompany
Good to Great

Why Some Companies
Make the Leap . . .
and Others Don't

JIM COLLINS

rh

BUSINESS
BOOKS

Published by Random House Business Books 2006

7 9 10 8

First published in the United Kingdom in 2006 by
Random House Business Books
First published in the United States in 2006 by Jim Collins

www.rbooks.co.uk

Addresses for companies within The Random House Group Limited can be
found at: www.randomhouse.co.uk/offices.htm

The Random House Group Limited Reg. No. 954009

A CIP catalogue record for this book
is available from the British Library

ISBN 9781905211326

The Random House Group Limited supports The Forest Stewardship
Council (FSC), the leading international forest certification organisation.
All our titles that are printed on Greenpeace approved FSC certified paper
carry the FSC logo. Our paper procurement policy can be found at
www.rbooks.co.uk/environment

Mixed Sources
Product group from well-managed
forests and other controlled sources
www.fsc.org Cert no. TT-COC-2139
© 1996 Forest Stewardship Council

Printed and bound in Great Britain by
Clays Ltd, St Ives PLC

During my first year on the Stanford faculty in 1988, I sought out emeritus professor John Gardner for guidance on how I might become a better teacher. Gardner, former Secretary of Health, Education and Welfare, founder of Common Cause, and author of the classic text *Self-Renewal*, stung me with a comment that changed my life.

"It occurs to me, Jim, that you spend too much time trying to be interesting," he said. "Why don't you invest more time being interested."

I don't know if this monograph will prove interesting to everyone who reads it, but I do know that it results from my growing interest in the social sectors. My interest began for two reasons. First is the surprising reach of our work into the social sectors. I'm generally categorized as a business author, yet a third or more of my readers come from non-business. Second is the sheer joy of learning something new—in this case, about the challenges facing social sector leaders—and puzzling over questions that arise from applying our work to circumstances quite different from business.

I originally intended this text to be a new chapter in future editions of *Good to Great*. But upon reflection, I concluded that it would be inappropriate to force my readers to buy a second copy of the book just to get access to this piece—and so we decided to create this independent monograph. That said, while this monograph can certainly be read as a stand-alone piece, I've written it to go hand-in-hand with the book, and the greatest value will accrue to those who read the two together.

I do not consider myself an expert on the social sectors, but in the spirit of John Gardner, I am a student. Yet I've become a passionate student. I've come to see that it is simply not good enough to focus solely on having a great business sector. If we only have great companies, we will merely have a prosperous society, not a great one. Economic growth and power are the means, not the definition, of a great nation.

Jim Collins
www.jimcollins.com
Boulder, Colorado
July 24, 2005

GOOD TO GREAT
AND THE SOCIAL SECTORS

Why Business Thinking Is Not the Answer

We must reject the idea—well-intentioned, but dead wrong—that the primary path to greatness in the social sectors is to become "more like a business." Most businesses—like most of anything else in life—fall somewhere between mediocre and good. Few are great. When you compare great companies with good ones, many widely practiced business norms turn out to correlate with mediocrity, not greatness. So, then, why would we want to import the practices of mediocrity into the social sectors?

I shared this perspective with a gathering of business CEOs, and offended nearly everyone in the room. A hand shot up from David Weekley, one of the more thoughtful CEOs—a man who built a very successful company and who now spends nearly half his time working with the social sectors. "Do you have evidence to support your point?" he demanded. "In my work with nonprofits, I find that they're in desperate need of greater discipline—disciplined planning, disciplined people, disciplined governance, disciplined allocation of resources."

"What makes you think that's a *business* concept?" I replied. "Most businesses *also* have a desperate need for greater discipline. Mediocre companies rarely display the relentless culture of discipline—disciplined people who engage in disciplined thought and who take disciplined action—that we find in truly great companies. A culture of discipline is not a principle of business; it is a principle of greatness."

Later, at dinner, we continued our debate, and I asked Weekley: "If you had taken a different path in life and become, say, a church leader, a university president, a nonprofit leader, a hospital CEO, or a school superintendent, would you have been any less disciplined in your approach? Would you have been less likely to practice enlightened leadership, or put less energy into getting the right people on the bus, or been less demanding of results?" Weekley considered the question for a long moment. "No, I suspect not."

> That's when it dawned on me: we need a new language. The critical distinction is not between business and social, but between great and good. We need to reject the naïve imposition of the "language of business" on the social sectors, and instead jointly embrace a *language of greatness.*

That's what our work is about: building a framework of greatness, articulating timeless principles that explain why some become great and others do not. We derived these principles from a rigorous matched-pair research method, comparing companies that became great with companies that did not. Our work is not fundamentally about business; it is about what separates great from good.

THE GOOD-TO-GREAT MATCHED-PAIR RESEARCH METHOD

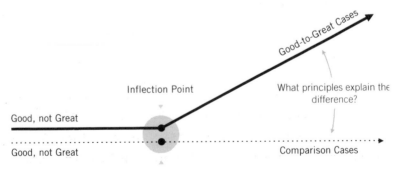

Social sector leaders have embraced this distinction—the principles of greatness, as distinct from the practices of business—with remarkable ease. If a nonbusiness reader is just as likely to email me as a business reader, then somewhere between 30% and 50% of those who have read *Good to Great* come from nonbusiness. We've received thousands of calls, letters, emails and invitations from education, healthcare, churches, the arts, social services, cause-driven nonprofits, police, government agencies, and even military units.

Two messages leap out. First, the good-to-great principles do indeed apply to the social sectors, perhaps even better than we expected. Second, particular questions crop up repeatedly from social sector leaders facing realities they perceive to be quite different from the business sector. I've synthesized these questions into five issues that form the framework of this piece:

1 - Defining "Great"—Calibrating Success without Business Metrics

2 - Level 5 Leadership—Getting Things Done within a Diffuse Power Structure

3 - First Who—Getting the Right People on the Bus within Social Sector Constraints

4 - The Hedgehog Concept—Rethinking the Economic Engine without a Profit Motive

5 - Turning the Flywheel—Building Momentum by Building the Brand

I've based this piece on critical feedback, structured interviews, and laboratory work with more than 100 social sector leaders. While I hope to eventually see the results of matched-pair research that uses non-business entities as the data set, such research studies—done right—require up to a decade to complete. In the meantime, I feel a responsibility to respond to the questions raised by those who seek to apply the good-to-great principles today, and I offer this monograph as a small interim step.

ISSUE ONE: DEFINING "GREAT"—CALIBRATING SUCCESS WITHOUT BUSINESS METRICS

In 1995, officers at the New York City Police Department (NYPD) found an anonymous note posted on the bulletin board. "We're not report takers," the note proclaimed. "We're the police."[1] The note testified to the psychological shift when then Police Commissioner William J. Bratton inverted the focus from inputs to outputs. Prior to Bratton, the NYPD assessed itself primarily on input variables—such as arrests made, reports taken, cases closed, budgets met—rather than on the output variable of reducing crime. Bratton set audacious output goals, such as attaining double-digit annual declines in felony crime rates, and implemented a catalytic mechanism called Compstat (short for "computer comparison statistics").

A 1996 *Time* article describes a police captain sweating at a podium in the command center. He stands before an overhead map with a bunch of red dots, showing a significant increase in robberies in his precinct. In a Socratic grilling session reminiscent of Professor Kingfield in *The Paper Chase*, the questions come relentlessly. "What is the pattern here?" "What are you going to do to take these guys out?"[2] According to *CIO Insight* magazine, 75% of commanders found themselves ejected from their positions for failing to reduce crime in their precincts. "If, week after week at the Compstat meetings, we found precinct commanders not performing to the standards," explained Bratton, "we had to find someone else to do the job."[3]

This distinction between inputs and outputs is fundamental, yet frequently missed. I recently opened the pages of a business magazine that rated charities based in part on the percentage of budget spent on management, overhead and fundraising. It's a well-intentioned idea, but reflects profound confusion between inputs and outputs. Think about it this way: If you rank collegiate athletic departments based on coaching salaries, you'd find that Stanford University has a higher coaching cost structure as a percentage of total expenses than some other Division I schools. Should we therefore rank Stanford as "less great"? Following the logic of the business magazine, that's what we might conclude—and our conclusion would be absurd. Stanford won the National Association of Collegiate Directors of Athletics Cup for best overall performance for 10 consecutive years, beating out all other major schools, while delivering athlete graduation rates above 80%.[4] To say, "Stanford is a less great program because it has a higher salary structure than some other schools" would miss the main point that Stanford Athletics delivered exceptional performance, defined by the bottom-line *outputs* of athletic and academic achievement.

> The confusion between inputs and outputs stems from one of the primary differences between business and the social sectors. In business, money is both an input (a resource for achieving greatness) *and* an output (a measure of greatness). In the social sectors, money is *only* an input, and not a measure of greatness.

A great organization is one that delivers superior performance and makes a distinctive impact over a long period of time. For a business, financial returns are a perfectly legitimate measure of performance. For a social sector organization, however, performance must be assessed relative to mission, not financial returns. In the social sectors, the critical question is not "How much money do we make per dollar of invested capital?" but "How effectively do we deliver on our mission and make a distinctive impact, relative to our resources?"

Now, you might be thinking, "OK, but collegiate sports programs and police departments have one giant advantage: you can measure win records and crime rates. What if your outputs are inherently *not* measurable?" The basic idea is still the same: separate inputs from outputs, and hold yourself accountable for progress in outputs, *even if those outputs defy measurement.*

When Tom Morris became executive director of The Cleveland Orchestra in 1987, the orchestra faced deficits exceeding 10%, a small and stagnant endowment, and a struggling local economy. Prior to taking the position, Morris asked two key board members, "What do you want me to do if I come here?" Their answer: make an already great orchestra even greater, defined by artistic excellence.

GREATNESS AT THE CLEVELAND ORCHESTRA

SUPERIOR PERFORMANCE	- Emotional response of audience; number of standing ovations increased.
	- Wide technical range: can play any piece with excellence, no matter how difficult—from soothing and familiar classical pieces to difficult and unfamiliar modern pieces.
	- Increased demand for tickets—even for more complex, imaginative programs—not just in Cleveland, but also when visiting New York and Europe.
	- Invited (and then reinvited, and reinvited again) to Salzburg Festival—for the first time in 25 years—signifying elite status with the top European orchestras.
DISTINCTIVE IMPACT	- The Cleveland style of programming increasingly copied and becoming more influential.
	- A key point of civic pride; cab drivers say, "We're really proud of our orchestra."
	- Severance Hall filled to capacity two nights after 9/11, as a place for the community to grieve together through the transformative power of great music.
	- Orchestra leaders increasingly sought for leadership roles and perspectives in elite industry groups/gatherings.
LASTING ENDURANCE	- Excellence sustained across generations of conductors—from George Szell through Pierre Boulez, Christoph-von Dohnányi, and Franz Welser-Möst.
	- Supporters donate time and money, investing in the long-term success of the orchestra; endowment tripled.
	- Strong organization before, during and after Tom Morris's tenure.

Tom Morris could not precisely measure artistic excellence, but that does not change the fact that artistic excellence *is* the primary definition of performance for The Cleveland Orchestra. Nor does it change the extreme discipline with which The Cleveland Orchestra held itself accountable for playing the most challenging classical music with supreme artistic excellence, and doing so even better with each passing year, guided by the BHAG (Big Hairy Audacious Goal) of becoming recognized as one of the three greatest orchestras in the world.

"We asked a simple question," explained Morris. "What do we mean by great results?" Morris and his team tracked a variety of indicators. Are we getting more standing ovations? Are we expanding the range of what we can play with perfection—from clean classical pieces to complex modern pieces? Are we invited to the most prestigious festivals in Europe? Are tickets in greater demand, not just in Cleveland, but when we play in New York? Do people increasingly mimic the Cleveland style of programming? Do composers increasingly seek to have their work debuted at Cleveland? Under Tom Morris, the orchestra tripled its endowment to $120 million (even accounting for the post-dotcom bubble decline in assets) and funded a remodel of Severance Hall into one of the best music halls anywhere. He accomplished this because he understood that endowment, revenues and cost structure were input variables, not the output variables of greatness.[5]

Clear, rigorous thinking is precisely what Cleveland's Tom Morris and New York's Commissioner Bratton brought to their work. They separated inputs from outputs, and had the discipline to hold their organizations accountable for achievement in the outputs. That Bratton had the advantage of quantitative metrics, and Morris did not, is largely beside the point.

> It doesn't really matter whether you can quantify your results. What matters is that you rigorously assemble *evidence*—quantitative or qualitative—to track your progress. If the evidence is primarily qualitative, think like a trial lawyer assembling the combined body of evidence. If the evidence is primarily quantitative, then think of yourself as a laboratory scientist assembling and assessing the data.

To throw our hands up and say, "But we cannot measure performance in the social sectors the way you can in a business" is simply lack of discipline. All indicators are flawed, whether qualitative or quantitative. Test scores are flawed, mammograms are flawed, crime data are flawed, customer service data are flawed, patient-outcome data are flawed. What matters is not finding the perfect indicator, but settling upon a *consistent and intelligent* method of assessing your output results, and then tracking your trajectory with rigor. What do you mean by great performance? Have you established a baseline? Are you improving? If not, why not? How can you improve even faster toward your audacious goals?

GOOD-TO-GREAT FRAMEWORK—INPUTS AND OUTPUTS OF GREATNESS

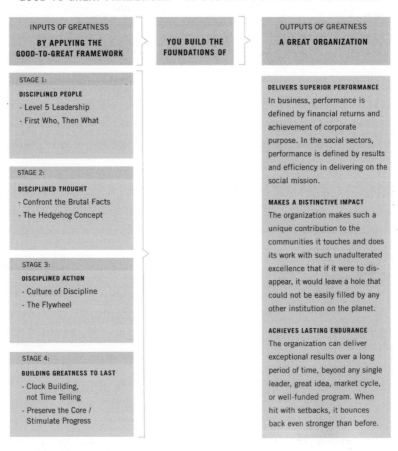

INPUTS OF GREATNESS

BY APPLYING THE GOOD-TO-GREAT FRAMEWORK

YOU BUILD THE FOUNDATIONS OF

OUTPUTS OF GREATNESS

A GREAT ORGANIZATION

STAGE 1:

DISCIPLINED PEOPLE
- Level 5 Leadership
- First Who, Then What

STAGE 2:

DISCIPLINED THOUGHT
- Confront the Brutal Facts
- The Hedgehog Concept

STAGE 3:

DISCIPLINED ACTION
- Culture of Discipline
- The Flywheel

STAGE 4:

BUILDING GREATNESS TO LAST
- Clock Building, not Time Telling
- Preserve the Core / Stimulate Progress

DELIVERS SUPERIOR PERFORMANCE
In business, performance is defined by financial returns and achievement of corporate purpose. In the social sectors, performance is defined by results and efficiency in delivering on the social mission.

MAKES A DISTINCTIVE IMPACT
The organization makes such a unique contribution to the communities it touches and does its work with such unadulterated excellence that if it were to disappear, it would leave a hole that could not be easily filled by any other institution on the planet.

ACHIEVES LASTING ENDURANCE
The organization can deliver exceptional results over a long period of time, beyond any single leader, great idea, market cycle, or well-funded program. When hit with setbacks, it bounces back even stronger than before.

You can think of the entire good-to-great framework as a generic set of input variables that correlate strongly with creating the outputs of greatness. (In the diagram "Good-to-Great Framework—Inputs and Outputs of Greatness" on page 8, I've summarized the idea, showing how disciplined application of the good-to-great principles leads to creating the outputs that define a great organization.) Any journey from good to great requires relentlessly adhering to these input variables, rigorously tracking your trajectory on the output variables, and then driving yourself to even higher levels of performance and impact. No matter how much you have achieved, *you will always be merely good relative to what you can become.* Greatness is an inherently dynamic process, not an end point. The moment you think of yourself as great, your slide toward mediocrity will have already begun.

ISSUE TWO: **LEVEL 5 LEADERSHIP—GETTING THINGS DONE WITHIN A DIFFUSE POWER STRUCTURE**

When Frances Hesselbein became CEO of the Girl Scouts of the USA, a *New York Times* columnist asked what it felt like to be on top of such a large organization. With patience, like a teacher pausing to impart an important lesson, Hesselbein proceeded to rearrange the lunch table, creating a set of concentric circles radiating outward—plates, cups, saucers—connected by knives, forks and spoons. Hesselbein pointed to a glass in the middle of the table. "I'm here," she said.[6] Hesselbein may have had the title of Chief Executive Officer, but her message was clear: *I'm not on top of anything.*

Facing a complex governance structure composed of hundreds of local Girl Scout councils (each with its own governing board) and a volunteer force of 650,000, Hesselbein simply did not have the full power of decision. Even so, she moved people to confront brutal facts facing girls in modern America, such as teen pregnancy and alcohol use, by creating materials on sensitive issues. Proficiency badges sprouted up in topics like math, technology and computer science, to reinforce the idea that girls are—and should think of themselves as—capable individuals who can take control of their own lives. Hesselbein did not force this change down people's throats, but simply gave the interdependent councils the opportunity to make changes at their own discretion. Most did.[7]

When asked how she got all this done without concentrated executive power, she said, "Oh, you always have power, if you just know where to find it. There is the power of inclusion, and the power of language, and the power of shared interests, and the power of coalition. Power is all around you to draw upon, but it is rarely raw, rarely visible." Whether they answer to a nonprofit board composed of prominent citizens, an elected school board, a governmental oversight mechanism, a set of trustees, a democratic religious congregation, an elected membership association or any number of other species of governance, social sector leaders face a complex and diffuse power map. When you add in tenured faculty, civil service, volunteers, police unions, or any number of other internal factors, most nonbusiness leaders simply do not have the concentrated decision power of a business CEO.

> Social sector leaders are not less decisive than business leaders as a general rule; they only appear that way to those who fail to grasp the complex governance and diffuse power structures common to social sectors. Frances Hesselbein was just as decisive as nearly any corporate CEO, but she faced a governance and power structure that rendered executive-style leadership impractical.

This is why some business executives fail when they move into the social sectors. One corporate CEO turned academic dean tried to lead faculty toward his vision. The more he brought to bear his executive skill, the more the faculty decided they had better things to do than to attend the dean's faculty meetings. After all, what was he going to do? Fire them? They all had tenure. After "one of the most draining experiences in my life," this CEO returned to the business world. He did not understand—until it was too late—what one university president called the reality of tenured faculty: "A thousand points of no."

The complex governance and diffuse power structures common in nonbusiness lead me to hypothesize that there are two types of leadership skill: *executive* and *legislative*. In executive leadership, the individual leader has enough concentrated power to simply make the right decisions. In legislative leadership, on the other hand, no individual leader—not even the nominal chief executive—has enough structural power to make the most important decisions by himself or herself. Legislative leadership relies more upon persuasion, political currency, and shared interests to create the conditions for the right decisions to happen. And it is precisely this legislative dynamic that makes Level 5 leadership particularly important to the social sectors.

Our good-to-great research uncovered that leadership capabilities follow a five-level hierarchy, with Level 5 at the top. Level 5 leaders differ from Level 4 leaders in that they are ambitious first and foremost for the cause, the movement, the mission, the work—*not themselves*—and they have the will to do whatever it takes (*whatever* it takes) to make good on that ambition. (See diagram: "Level 5 Leadership" on page 12.) In the social sectors, the Level 5's compelling combination of personal humility and professional will is a key factor in creating legitimacy and influence. After all, why should those over whom you have no direct power give themselves over to a decision that is primarily about you? As one social sector leader confided, "I've learned that Level 5 leadership requires being clever for the greater good. In the end, it is my responsibility to ensure that the right decisions happen—even if I don't have the sole power to make those decisions, and even if those decisions could not win a popular vote. The only way I can achieve that is if people know that I'm motivated first and always for the greatness of our work, not myself."

> Level 5 leadership is not about being "soft" or "nice" or purely "inclusive" or "consensus-building." The whole point of Level 5 is to make sure the *right* decisions happen—no matter how difficult or painful— for the long-term greatness of the institution and the achievement of its mission, independent of consensus or popularity.

LEVEL 5 LEADERSHIP / LEVEL 5 HIERARCHY

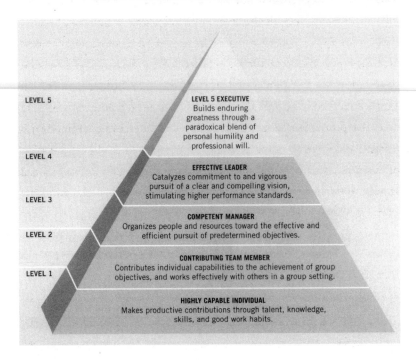

LEVEL 5

LEVEL 5 EXECUTIVE
Builds enduring greatness through a paradoxical blend of personal humility and professional will.

LEVEL 4

EFFECTIVE LEADER
Catalyzes commitment to and vigorous pursuit of a clear and compelling vision, stimulating higher performance standards.

LEVEL 3

COMPETENT MANAGER
Organizes people and resources toward the effective and efficient pursuit of predetermined objectives.

LEVEL 2

CONTRIBUTING TEAM MEMBER
Contributes individual capabilities to the achievement of group objectives, and works effectively with others in a group setting.

LEVEL 1

HIGHLY CAPABLE INDIVIDUAL
Makes productive contributions through talent, knowledge, skills, and good work habits.

The executive versus legislative distinction remains a working hypothesis, awaiting rigorous research. If empirical evidence validates the distinction, it is unlikely to be as simple as "business sector = executive" and "social sectors = legislative." More likely, there will be a spectrum, and the most effective leaders will show a blend of *both* executive and legislative skills. The best leaders of the future—in the social sectors *and* business—will not be purely executive or legislative; they will have a knack for knowing when to play their executive chips, and when not to.

There is an irony in all this. Social sector organizations increasingly look to business for leadership models and talent, yet I suspect we will find more true leadership in the social sectors than the business sector. How can I say that? Because, as George MacGregor Burns taught in his classic 1978 text, *Leadership*, the practice of leadership is not the same as the exercise of power.[8] If I put a loaded gun to your head, I can get you to do things you might not otherwise do, but I've not practiced leadership; I've exercised power. *True leadership only exists if people follow when they have the freedom not to.* If people follow you because they have no choice, then you are not leading. Today's business leaders face highly mobile knowledge workers. They face Sarbanes-Oxley, environmental and consumer groups, and shareholder activists. In short, business executives don't have the same concentration of pure executive power they once enjoyed. Level 5 leadership combined with legislative skill will become even more important to the next generation of business executives, and they would do well to learn from the social sectors. Indeed, perhaps tomorrow's great business leaders will come from the social sectors, not the other way around.

ISSUE THREE: **FIRST WHO—GETTING THE RIGHT PEOPLE ON THE BUS, WITHIN SOCIAL SECTOR CONSTRAINTS**

In 1976, 25-year-old Roger Briggs began teaching physics at a suburban public high school in Boulder, Colorado. As he settled into daily teaching, a persistent thought pushed to the front of his consciousness, like a pebble inside a shoe: *Our schools could be so much better.*

But what could he do? He wasn't principal. He wasn't superintendent. He wasn't governor. Roger Briggs wanted to remain on the front line of education, shoulder to shoulder with fellow teachers. After becoming department chair, Briggs decided to turn his little arena into a pocket of greatness. "I rejected the idea of being just a member of the 'worker class,' accepting good as good enough. I couldn't change the whole system, but I could change our 14-person science department."

He began the same way all the good-to-great leaders began: First get the right people on the bus. Given the low compensation for teachers and the paucity of incentives, Briggs had to fill faculty seats with people compulsively driven to make whatever they touch the best it can be—not because of what they would "get" for it, but because they simply could not stop themselves from the almost neurotic need to improve. With a teachers' union that protected the mediocre and excellent alike, Briggs knew it would be more difficult to get the wrong people off the bus, so he focused instead on getting the right people *on* the bus. He began to view the first three years of a teacher's career as an extended interview. He inverted the three-year tenure recommendation from a default of "Yes, you'll likely get tenure, unless you've done something egregious" to a default of "No, you will most likely *not* get tenure, unless you have proven yourself to be an exceptional teacher."

A turning point came when an adequate teacher came up for tenure. "He was a good teacher, but not a great one," explained Briggs. "And I just felt we couldn't accept merely 'good' for our department." Briggs argued against granting tenure, and held firm to his countercultural position. Soon thereafter, a spectacular young teacher became available, and the science department hired her. "Had we tenured the other teacher, we'd have a good person in that seat, whereas now we have a great teacher," explained Briggs. As the culture of discipline tightened, the wrong teachers found themselves to be viruses surrounded by antibodies, and some self-ejected. The science department minibus changed—hire by hire and tenure decision by tenure decision—until a critical mass coalesced into a culture of discipline.[9]

The Roger Briggs story highlights three main points. First, and most important, you can build a pocket of greatness without executive power, in the middle of an organization. If Roger Briggs can lead his minibus from good to great within the constraints of the public school system, you can do it nearly anywhere. Second, you start by focusing on the First Who principle—do whatever you can to get the right people on the bus, the wrong people off the bus, and the right people into the right seats. Tenure poses one set of challenges, volunteers and lack of resources another, but the fact remains: greatness flows first and foremost from having the right people in the key seats, not the other way around. Third, Briggs accomplished all this with the use of early-assessment mechanisms, rigorously employed.

In the social sectors, where getting the wrong people off the bus can be more difficult than in a business, early assessment mechanisms turn out to be more important than hiring mechanisms. There is no perfect interviewing technique, no ideal hiring method; even the best executives make hiring mistakes. You can only know for certain about a person by working with that person.

Business executives can more easily fire people and—equally important—they can use money to buy talent. Most social sector leaders, on the other hand, must rely on people underpaid relative to the private sector or, in the case of volunteers, paid not at all. Yet a finding from our research is instructive: the key variable is not how (or how much) you pay, but *who* you have on the bus. The comparison companies in our research—those that failed to become great—placed greater emphasis on using incentives to "motivate" otherwise unmotivated or undisciplined people. The great companies, in contrast, focused on getting and hanging on to the right people in the first place—those who are productively neurotic, those who are *self*-motivated and *self*-disciplined, those who wake up every day, compulsively driven to do the best they can because it is simply part of their DNA. In the social sectors, when big incentives (or compensation at all, in the case of volunteers) are simply not possible, the First Who principle becomes even more important. Lack of resources is no excuse for lack of rigor—it makes selectivity all the more vital.

In the spring of 1988, Wendy Kopp graduated from Princeton with an elegant idea: why not convince graduates from leading universities to spend the first two years of their careers teaching low-income kids in the public education system? She had no money, no office, no infrastructure, no name, no credibility, no furniture, not even a bed or a dresser in which to store her clothes. In her book, *One Day, All Children . . .* , Kopp tells of moving into a small room in New York City after graduation, plopping her sleeping bag on the floor and pulling jeans and shirts out of three garbage bags and piling them into neat stacks on the floor. After convincing Mobil Corporation to grant $26,000 of seed capital to found Teach for America, Kopp spent the next 365 days in a juggling act—convincing top-flight people to join her bus with the promise that she would convince donors to fund the bus, while at the same time convincing donors that she would convince top-flight people to join her bus.

One year later, Kopp stood in front of 500 recent-graduates from colleges like Yale, Harvard and Michigan, assembled for training and deployment into America's underserved classrooms. And how did she convince these graduates to work for low pay in tough classrooms? First, by tapping their idealistic passions, and second, by making the process *selective*. "She basically said to all these overachieving college students: 'If you're really good, you might be able to join our cause,'" explained Michael Brown of City Year, who watched with admiration. " 'But first, you have to submit to a rigorous screening and evaluation process. You should prepare yourself for rejection, because it takes a special capability to succeed in these classrooms.' "[10]

Selectivity led to credibility with donors, which increased funding, which made it possible to attract and select even more young people into the program. As of 2005, more than 97,000 individuals applied to be part of Teach for America (yes, *ninety-seven thousand*), and only 14,100 made the cut, while revenues grew to nearly $40 million in annual support.[11]

Wendy Kopp understood three fundamental points. First, the more selective the process, the more attractive a position becomes—even if volunteer or low pay. Second, the social sectors have one compelling advantage: desperate craving for meaning in our lives. Purity of mission—be it about educating young people, connecting people to God, making our cities safe, touching the soul with great art, feeding the hungry, serving the poor, or protecting our freedom—has the power to ignite passion and commitment. Third, *the* number-one resource for a great social sector organization is having enough of the right people willing to commit themselves to mission. The right people can often attract money, but money *by itself* can never attract the right people. Money is a commodity; talent is not. Time and talent can often compensate for lack of money, but money cannot ever compensate for lack of the right people.

ISSUE FOUR: **THE HEDGEHOG CONCEPT—RETHINKING THE ECONOMIC ENGINE WITHOUT A PROFIT MOTIVE**

The pivot point in *Good to Great* is the Hedgehog Concept. The essence of a Hedgehog Concept is to attain piercing clarity about how to produce the best long-term results, and then exercising the relentless discipline to say, "No thank you" to opportunities that fail the hedgehog test. When we examined the Hedgehog Concepts of the good-to-great companies, we found they reflected deep understanding of three intersecting circles: 1) what you are deeply passionate about, 2) what you can be the best in the world at, and 3) what best drives your economic engine.

Social sector leaders found the Hedgehog Concept helpful, but many rebelled against the third circle, the economic engine. I found this puzzling. Sure, making money is not the point, but you still need to have an economic engine to fulfill your mission.

Then I had a conversation with John Morgan, a pastor with more than 30 years of experience in congregational work, then serving as a minister of a church in Reading, Pennsylvania. "We're a congregation of misfits," said Morgan, "and I found the idea of a unifying Hedgehog Concept to be very helpful. We're passionate about trying to rebuild this community, and we can be the best in our region at creating a generation of transformational leaders that reflects the full diversity of the community. That is our Hedgehog Concept."

And what about the economic engine?

"Oh, we had to change that circle," he said. "It just doesn't make sense in a church."

"How can it not make sense," I pressed. "Don't you need to fund your work?"

"Well, there are two problems. First, we face a cultural problem of talking about money in a religious setting, coming from a tradition that says love of money is the root of all evil."

"But money is also the root of paying the light and phone bills," I said.

"True," said Morgan, "but you've got to keep in mind the deep discomfort of talking explicitly about money in some church settings. And second, we rely upon much more than money to keep this place going. How do we get enough resources of *all* types—not just money to pay the bills, but also time, emotional commitment, hands, hearts, and minds?"[12]

> Morgan put his finger on a fundamental difference between the business and social sectors. The third circle of the Hedgehog Concept shifts from being an economic engine to a *resource* engine. The critical question is not "How much money do we make?" but "How can we develop a sustainable resource engine to deliver superior performance relative to our mission?"

In looking across a range of social sector organizations, I submit that the resource engine has three basic components: time, money and brand. "Time"—the subject of the previous section—refers to how well you attract people willing to contribute their efforts for free, or at rates below what their talents would yield in business (First Who!). "Money"—the subject of this section—refers to sustained cash flow. "Brand"—the subject of the next section—refers to how well your organization can cultivate a deep well of emotional goodwill and mindshare of potential supporters. (See diagram: "The Hedgehog Concept in the Social Sectors" on page 19.)

In *Good to Great*, we uncovered the idea of the "economic denominator." If you could pick only one ratio—profit per *x*—to systematically increase over time, what "*x*" would have the most significant impact on your economic engine? This economic ratio ties perfectly to the economic core in all businesses, namely the profit mechanism, translated into return on invested capital.

THE HEDGEHOG CONCEPT IN THE SOCIAL SECTORS

Circle 1: **Passion** - Understanding what your organization stands for (its core values) and why it exists (its mission or core purpose).

Circle 2: **Best at** - Understanding what your organization can uniquely contribute to the people it touches, better than any other organization on the planet.

Circle 3: **Resource Engine** - Understanding what best drives your resource engine, broken into three parts: time, money, and brand.

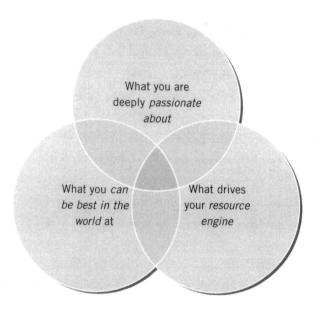

The same idea does not translate to the social sectors. For one thing, as Tom Tierney of The Bridgespan Group aptly observed, the social sectors do not have rational capital markets that channel resources to those who deliver the best results. For another, there is no one underlying economic driver—the analogy to profit per "x"—that applies across all social sector organizations. The whole purpose of the social sectors is to meet social objectives, human needs and national priorities that *cannot* be priced at a profit.

We examined the economic components of 44 non-business organizations, across a range of arenas. Using budget statements, annual reports, financial statements, and IRS Form 990s, Michael Lane on my research team collated the information into sources of funds, expense categories, restricted versus unrestricted assets, and executive compensation. While our analysis was limited in scope and modest in ambition, we nonetheless found the data illuminating.

If you place social sector entities in a two-by-two matrix, with one axis representing charitable donations and private grants and the other axis representing business revenue (fee for service, contracts, products, etc.), we find social sector organizations spread widely across all four quadrants. (See "Economic Engine in the Social Sectors: 4 Quadrants" on page 21.) Even institutions in the same "industry" can fall into different economic quadrants. Girl Scouts councils, for instance, derive substantial cash flow from selling Girl Scout Cookies®, and almost none from government support[13]; the Boys & Girls Clubs of America, in contrast, derives more than half its revenue from government support. Furthermore, each economic quadrant demands its own unique skills. Those that rely on government funding must employ political skill and cultivate public support; NASA, for instance, must convince Congress that it merits a budget that would place it high on the list of *Fortune* 500 corporations. Those that rely on charitable donations, on the other hand, must develop fundraising mechanisms and build emotional connection—"helping to cure cancer will make you feel good"—whereas those that rely heavily on business revenues, such as hospitals, more closely resemble the economic dynamics of a business corporation.

Yet the wide variation in economic structures in the social sectors increases the importance of the hedgehog principle—the inherent complexity requires deeper, more penetrating insight and rigorous clarity than in your average business entity. You begin with passion, then you refine passion with a rigorous assessment of what you can best contribute to the communities you touch. Then you create a way to tie your resource engine directly to the other two circles.

ECONOMIC ENGINE IN
THE SOCIAL SECTORS:
4 QUADRANTS

Quadrant I: This is the heavily government-funded quadrant. Organizations such as NASA, the United States Marine Corps, K-12 public education, charter schools, police departments, and other government-funded agencies fall into this quadrant. The quadrant also includes nonprofits that rely substantially on direct government support to augment their other revenue sources, such as the Boys & Girls Clubs. The resource engine in this quadrant depends heavily on political skill and maintaining public support.

Quadrant II: This quadrant relies heavily upon charitable support by private individuals. Many cause-driven nonprofits fall into this category—such as the American Cancer Society, the Special Olympics, and Habitat for Humanity—as do many religious institutions, community foundations, and local charities. The resource engine in this quadrant depends heavily on personal relationships and excellent fundraising.

Quadrant III: This hybrid quadrant consists of those that blend charitable donations with business revenues. Performing arts organizations gravitate toward this quadrant, along with organizations that have created a unique business revenue stream to augment the economic component of the resource engine, such as local Girl Scouts councils with their cookie businesses and Share Our Strength with its corporate sponsorship business. This quadrant requires both business acumen *and* fundraising skill.

Quadrant IV: This quadrant captures those that rely heavily on a business revenue stream. Organizations that fund themselves primarily through products, services, tuition, contracts and so forth populate this quadrant. Many nonprofit hospitals fall into this quadrant as do many higher education institutions. It also includes a surprising number of traditional nonprofits, such as the Red Cross with its $2 billion biomedical services business (principally blood products) and Goodwill Industries with its thrift stores. The resource engine in this quadrant most closely resembles that of a for-profit business.

> The critical step in the Hedgehog Concept is to determine how best to connect all three circles, so that they reinforce each other. You must be able to answer the question, "How does focusing on what we can do best tie directly to our resource engine, and how does our resource engine directly reinforce what we can do best?" And you must be right.

When Drew Buscareno became executive director of the Center for the Homeless in South Bend, Indiana, he and his team developed a distinct Hedgehog Concept. They believed the Center could become the best in the world at breaking the cycle of homelessness in Bibletowns of the Midwest by challenging homeless people to take responsibility for their own lives. They soon realized that building a resource engine primarily around government funding would run counter to the Center's Hedgehog Concept.

"Homelessness is a profound disconnectedness from self, family and community," explained Buscareno. "This insight fueled everything we did. We organized our whole organization around connecting people—homeless people, benefactors, volunteers, and staff—to self, family and community. Aggressively pursuing government money does not make any sense with this type of thinking, but aggressively connecting volunteers and local donors on a personal level with homeless people makes absolute sense."

The Center built its economic engine around individuals who give five or ten thousand dollars a year consistently, and who personally connect to the Center's mission. As of 2004, less than 10% of the Center's resource engine came from government—not because government funding was unavailable, but because such funding largely did not fit with the other two circles of the Center's Hedgehog Concept.[14]

As Peter Drucker admonished, the foundation for doing good is doing well. To which I would add that the foundation for doing well lies in a relentless focus on your Hedgehog Concept. The old adage "no cash flow, no mission" is true, but only as part of a larger truth. A great social sector organization must have the discipline to say, "No thank you" to resources that drive it away from the middle of its three circles. Those who have the discipline to attract and channel resources directed solely at their Hedgehog Concept, *and to reject resources that drive them away from the center of their three circles*, will be of greater service to the world.

ISSUE FIVE: **TURNING THE FLYWHEEL—BUILDING MOMENTUM BY BUILDING THE BRAND**

In building a great institution, there is no single defining action, no grand program, no one killer innovation, no solitary lucky break, no miracle moment. Rather, our research showed that it feels like turning a giant, heavy flywheel. Pushing with great effort—days, weeks and months of work, with almost imperceptible progress—you finally get the flywheel to inch forward. But you don't stop. You keep pushing, and with persistent effort, you eventually get the flywheel to complete one entire turn. You don't stop. You keep pushing, in an intelligent and consistent direction, and the flywheel moves a bit faster. You keep pushing, and you get two turns ... then four ... then eight ... the flywheel builds momentum ... sixteen ... you keep pushing ... thirty two ... it builds more momentum ... a hundred ... moving faster with each turn ... a thousand ... ten thousand ... a hundred thousand. Then, at some point—breakthrough! Each turn builds upon previous work, compounding your investment of effort. The flywheel flies forward with almost unstoppable momentum. This is how you build greatness.

By focusing on your Hedgehog Concept, you build results. Those results, in turn, attract resources and commitment, which you use to build a strong organization. That strong organization then delivers even better results, which attracts greater resources and commitment, which builds a stronger organization, which enables even better results. People want to feel the excitement of being involved in something that just flat out works. When they begin to see tangible results—when they can *feel* the flywheel beginning to build speed—that's when most people line up to throw their shoulders against the wheel and push.

> This is the power of the flywheel. Success breeds support and commitment, which breeds even greater success, which breeds more support and commitment—round *and* around the flywheel goes. People like to support winners!

In the business sector, the flywheel works exceptionally well. Deliver superior financial results, and the world will line up, eager to give you capital. In the social sectors, by contrast, there is no guaranteed relationship between exceptional results and sustained access to resources. In fact, the exact *opposite* can happen. As Clara Miller shows in her superb article, "Hidden in Plain Sight" (*Nonprofit Quarterly*, Spring 2003), nonprofit funding tends to favor programmatic funding, not building great organizations: "If you have a surplus, why should I give you a grant?" Small nonprofits face a valley of the shadow of death in making the shift from programmatic funding to sustained, unrestricted funding, and many fail along the way.

I find it puzzling how people who clearly understand the idea of investing in great companies run by the right people often fail to carry the same logic over to the social sectors. In place of the "fair-price exchange" of the free-market model, those who fund the social sectors can bring an assumption of "fair exchange" that is highly dysfunctional: if we give you money, we are entitled to tell you how to use that money, since it was a gift (or public funding), not a fair-price exchange. Put another way, social sector funding often favors "time telling"— focusing on a specific program or restricted gift, often the brainchild of a charismatic visionary leader. But building a great organization requires a shift to "clock building"—shaping a strong, self-sustaining organization that can prosper beyond any single programmatic idea or visionary leader. Restricted giving misses a fundamental point: to make the greatest impact on society requires first and foremost a great organization, not a single great program. If an institution has a focused Hedgehog Concept and a disciplined organization that delivers exceptional results, the best thing supporters can do is to give resources that enable the institution's leaders *to do their work the best way they know how.* Get out of their way, and let them build a clock!

Yet despite the differences between business and social sector economics, those who lead institutions from good to great must harness the flywheel effect. Whereas in business, the key driver in the flywheel is the link between financial success and capital resources, I'd like to suggest that a key link in the social sectors is brand reputation—built upon tangible results and emotional share of heart—so that potential supporters believe not only in your mission, but in your capacity to deliver on that mission.

Does Harvard truly deliver a better education and do better academic work than other universities? Perhaps, but the emotional pull of Harvard overcomes any doubt when it comes to raising funds. Despite having an endowment in excess of $20 billion, donations continue to flow.[15] As one Harvard graduate put it, "I give money to Harvard every year, and sometimes I feel like I'm bringing sand to the beach." Does the Red Cross truly do the best job of disaster relief? Perhaps, but the brand reputation of the Red Cross gives people an easy answer to the question, "How can I help?" when a disaster hits. Is the American Cancer Society the best mechanism for conquering cancer, or the Nature Conservancy the most effective at protecting the environment? Perhaps, but their brand reputations give people an easy way to support a cause they care about. The same applies to government-funded entities. NYPD has a brand. The United States Marine Corps has a brand. NASA has a brand. Anyone seeking to cut funding must contend with the brand.

THE FLYWHEEL
IN THE SOCIAL SECTORS

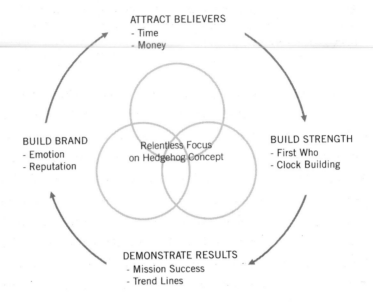

ATTRACT BELIEVERS
- Time
- Money

BUILD BRAND
- Emotion
- Reputation

Relentless Focus
on Hedgehog Concept

BUILD STRENGTH
- First Who
- Clock Building

DEMONSTRATE RESULTS
- Mission Success
- Trend Lines

In future research, we hope to test and gain deeper insight into the role of brand reputation in social sector organizations. (In the meantime, I recommend David Aaker's classic book, *Managing Brand Equity*.) But whatever this research might yield, I remain confident the flywheel effect will hold. Consistency distinguishes the truly great—consistent intensity of effort, consistency with the Hedgehog Concept, consistency with core values, consistency over time. Enduring great institutions practice the principle of Preserve the Core and Stimulate Progress, separating core values and fundamental purpose (which should never change) from mere operating practices, cultural norms and business strategies (which endlessly adapt to a changing world). Remaining true to your core values and focused on your Hedgehog Concept means, above all, rigorous clarity not just about what to do, but equally, what to *not* do.

Social sector leaders pride themselves on "doing good" for the world, but to be of maximum service requires a ferocious focus on doing good *only* if it fits with your Hedgehog Concept. To do the most good requires saying "no" to pressures to stray, and the discipline to stop doing what does not fit.

On Tuesday, September 11, 2001, the Cleveland Orchestra prepared for Thursday's concert, rehearsing Mahler's Fifth Symphony. As the magnitude of the terrorist attacks became clear, orchestra members put down their instruments and stopped rehearsal for the day. The next morning, Tom Morris and music director Christoph von Dohnányi debated what to do about Thursday's concert. They could cancel, just like nearly every other public event in America that week. Or they could go ahead with a concert, but if so, what should the orchestra play? Already, Morris had sensed mounting pressure from members of the community to abandon the classical repertoire in favor of a purely American program for the entire evening.

Morris and Dohnányi concluded that, perhaps more than any other week in history, people needed the orchestra to do the one thing it does supremely well: play the most powerful orchestral music ever created by the human race. They decided to go ahead with Mahler's Fifth—a piece inspired by the extreme emotions of death, love and life. Mahler's Fifth begins with a desolate funeral march announced by solo trumpet, joined by cataclysmic onslaughts from the full orchestra, and ends 65 minutes later with a cathartic celebration of birth and renewal. It's almost as if Mahler had written the piece *after* 9/11, not 100 years before, to console the soul of a nation shot right through the heart.

As Severance Hall filled on the evening of September 13th—every seat taken—people received a slip of paper with the simple message, "Tonight's concert will begin with a moment of silence." At precisely 8 p.m., Christoph von Dohnányi, tall and regal with a striking mane of white hair, strode onto stage, dressed in his conservative black tails. He turned to face the audience and began a moment of silence. Only it wasn't just a moment. Dohnányi carried the silence long past a minute, perhaps two, right to the point where five seconds more would have been five seconds too long. Then, he looked up. He turned to the orchestra, and waited a moment for everyone to sit down. The conductor raised his baton, paused, and then with the flick of his wrist shattered the silence with the opening trumpet salvo of Mahler 5.

"There is absolutely nothing we could have done to be of better service at that moment than to stick with what we do best, standing firm behind our core values of great music delivered with uncompromising artistic excellence," reflected Tom Morris.[16] It didn't matter that some patrons might want a rousing sing-along, or that others felt the orchestra should not play at all. It didn't matter that some might choose not to donate in the coming year, or that the media might criticize. What mattered is that the orchestra remained true to its core values and Hedgehog Concept, doing for the people of Cleveland *only* what it could do better than any other organization in the world.

BUILD A POCKET OF GREATNESS

Do you know which company attained the number-one spot in terms of return to investors on a dollar-for-dollar basis, of all U.S. publicly traded companies from 1972 to 2002? It's not GE. Not Intel. Not even Wal-Mart. Who came out number one? According to a 30-year analysis in *Money Magazine*, the winner is Southwest Airlines.[17]

Think about that for a minute. You cannot imagine a worse industry than airlines over this 30-year period: fuel shocks, deregulation, brutal competition, labor strife, 9/11, huge fixed costs, bankruptcy after bankruptcy after bankruptcy. And yet, according to *Money Magazine* calculations, a $10,000 investment in Southwest in 1972 would have returned more than $10 *million* by 2002. Meanwhile, United fell into bankruptcy, American limped along, and the airline industry remained one of the worst imaginable. Not only that, airlines that had the same model as Southwest got killed along the way. Airline executives have habitually blamed industry circumstances, ignoring the fact that the number-one best-performing investment in the universe of American public companies over a 30-year period is—just like them— an airline.

Now, consider a question: What if the people at Southwest had said, "Hey, we can't do anything great until we fix the systemic constraints facing the airline industry."?

I've conducted a large number of Socratic teaching sessions in the social sectors, and I've encountered an interesting dynamic: people often obsess on systemic constraints.

At a gathering of nonprofit healthcare leaders, I innocently asked, "What needs to happen for you to build great hospitals?"

"The Medicare system is broken, and it needs to be fixed," said one.

"Those who pay—insurers, the government, companies—are not the consumers, and this produces a fundamental problem," said another. "Everyone believes they are entitled to world-class healthcare, but no one wants to pay for it. And 40 million people have no insurance."

The group poured out a litany of constraints. "Doctors are both competitors and partners." "Fear of lawsuits." "The specter of health-care reform."

I put them in discussion groups, with the assignment to come up with at least one healthcare organization that made a leap to sustained and superior results. The groups dutifully went to work, and most came up with at least one solid example. Next, I said: "Now go back into your groups, and for each of your positive cases, try to identify an organ-ization that faced comparable circumstances—location, demographics, size, and so forth—but that did *not* make the leap." The groups went to work, and for the most part identified candidates. "So," I asked, "how do we explain the fact that some healthcare organizations made a breakthrough, while others facing similar (if not identical) systemic constraints did not?"

What would have happened if Roger Briggs in his science depart-ment, Tom Morris at the Cleveland Orchestra, William Bratton at the NYPD, Wendy Kopp of Teach for America, or Frances Hesselbein at the

Girl Scouts had all given up hope, thrown up their hands, and waited for the system to get fixed? It might take decades to change the entire systemic context, and you might be retired or dead by the time those changes come. In the meantime, what are you going to do *now*? This is where the Stockdale Paradox comes into play: You must retain faith that you can prevail to greatness in the end, while retaining the discipline to confront the brutal facts of your current reality. What can you do *today* to create a pocket of greatness, despite the brutal facts of your environment?

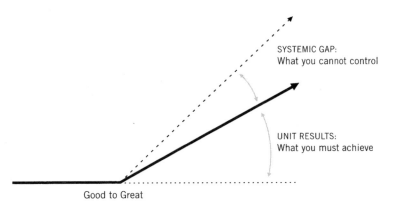

SYSTEMIC GAP:
What you cannot control

UNIT RESULTS:
What you must achieve

Good to Great

In the two summary tables that come at the end of this piece on pages 32-35, I've summarized the differences between the business and social sectors through the lens of the good-to-great framework. Both business leaders and social sector leaders face difficulties and constraints, but on net, I conclude that the relative advantages and disadvantages more or less cancel each other out. Great business corporations share more in common with great social sector organizations than they share with mediocre businesses. And the same holds in reverse. Again, the key question is not business versus social, but great versus good.

I do not mean to discount the systemic factors facing the social sectors. They are significant, and they must be addressed. Still, the fact remains, we can find pockets of greatness in nearly every difficult environment—whether it be the airline industry, education, healthcare, social ventures, or government-funded agencies. Every institution has its unique set of irrational and difficult constraints, yet some make a leap while others *facing the same environmental challenges* do not. This is perhaps the single most important point in all of *Good to Great*. Greatness is not a function of circumstance. Greatness, it turns out, is largely a matter of conscious choice, and discipline.

SUMMARY DIFFERENCES BETWEEN BUSINESS AND SOCIAL SECTORS
THROUGH THE GOOD-TO-GREAT FRAMEWORK

GOOD-TO-GREAT CONCEPT	BUSINESS SECTOR	SOCIAL SECTORS
Defining and Measuring "Great"	Widely agreed-upon financial metrics of performance. Money is both an input (a means to success) and an output (a measure of success).	Fewer widely agreed-upon metrics of performance. Money is only an input, not an output. Performance relative to mission, not financial returns, is the primary definition of success.
Level 5 Leadership	Governance structure and hierarchy relatively clear and straightforward. Concentrated and clear executive power. Can often substitute the use of power for the practice of leadership.	Governance structures often have more components and inherent ambiguity. More diffuse and less clear executive power. True leadership more prevalent, when defined as getting people to follow when they have the freedom not to.
First Who—Get the Right People on the Bus	Harder to tap the idealistic passions of people and to secure their full creative commitment for reasons beyond money. Often have substantial resources to attract and retain talent. Can more easily get the wrong people off the bus for poor performance.	One giant advantage: can more easily tap idealistic passions of people who seek nobility of service and meaning beyond money. Yet often lack the resources to acquire and retain talent. Tenure systems and volunteer dynamics can complicate getting the wrong people off the bus.
Confront the Brutal Facts—Living the Stockdale Paradox	Competitive market pressures force failing businesses to confront the brutal facts. Deep faith that the capitalist system basically works, and that the best performers will prevail in the end.	Often a culture of "niceness" that inhibits candor about the brutal facts. Systemic constraints can erode faith in the ability to prevail in the end—"Until we fix the system, we can't become great."

GOOD-TO-GREAT CONCEPT	BUSINESS SECTOR	SOCIAL SECTORS
Hedgehog Concept— Getting Your Three Circles Right	Economic engine tied directly to the profit mechanism; need only deliver to society items that can be priced at a profit. All businesses have the same fundamental economic driver: return on invested capital, connected to an underlying profit ratio—profit per "x."	Exist to meet social and human needs that cannot be priced at a profit. Third circle in Hedgehog Concept shifts from an economic engine to a *resource* engine composed of time, money and brand. Economic drivers vary across the social sectors; there is no one economic ratio.
Culture of Discipline	The profit mechanism makes it easier to say "no" or to stop doing that which does not fit the Hedgehog Concept. Pressures for growth, executive greed and short-term financial pressures can drive toward undisciplined behavior.	The desire to "do good" and the personal desires of donors and funders can drive to undisciplined decisions. Yet face less pressure for growth-for-growth's-sake, and generally less executive greed that might drive undisciplined decisions.
Flywheel, not Doom Loop	Efficient capital markets that connect to the profit mechanism. Results attract capital resources, which—in turn—enable results, which—in turn—create resources, which fuel greater results. . . round and around the flywheel goes.	No efficient capital markets to channel resources systematically to those who deliver the best results. Even so, the flywheel effect can still be harnessed by those who demonstrate success and build a brand. People like to support winners.
Clock Building, not Time Telling	The profit-driven economic engine makes it possible to create a sustained machine independent of any single leader or funding source.	Funding often favors "time telling" tied to specific projects or a charismatic leader, rather than to building a sustainable organization.
Preserve the Core / Stimulate Progress	Competitive pressures stimulate change and progress, yet make it harder to preserve core values. Easy-to-measure business metrics and trend lines to assess success and stimulate progress.	Passion for mission and core values a significant advantage, but can also make it harder to change traditions and sacred practices. Fewer easy-to-measure metrics to assess success and stimulate progress.

GOOD-TO-GREAT FRAMEWORK—CONCEPT SUMMARY

Our research shows that building a great organization proceeds in four basic stages; each stage consists of two fundamental principles*:

STAGE 1: DISCIPLINED PEOPLE

Level 5 Leadership. Level 5 leaders are ambitious first and foremost for the cause, the organization, the work—not themselves—and they have the fierce resolve to do whatever it takes to make good on that ambition. A Level 5 leader displays a paradoxical blend of personal humility and professional will.

First Who ... Then What. Those who build great organizations make sure they have the right people on the bus, the wrong people off the bus, and the right people in the key seats *before* they figure out where to drive the bus. They always think *first* about "who" and *then* about what.

STAGE 2: DISCIPLINED THOUGHT

Confront the Brutal Facts—The Stockdale Paradox. Retain unwavering faith that you can and will prevail in the end, regardless of the difficulties, *and at the same time* have the discipline to confront the most brutal facts of your current reality, whatever they might be.

The Hedgehog Concept. Greatness comes about by a series of good decisions consistent with a simple, coherent concept—a Hedgehog Concept. The Hedgehog Concept is an operating model that reflects understanding of three intersecting circles: what you can be the best in the world at, what you are deeply passionate about, and what best drives your economic or resource engine.

STAGE 3: DISCIPLINED ACTION

Culture of Discipline. Disciplined people who engage in disciplined thought and who take disciplined action—operating with freedom within a framework of responsibilities—this is the cornerstone of a culture that creates greatness. In a culture of discipline, people do not have jobs; they have *responsibilities*.

The Flywheel. In building greatness, there is no single defining action, no grand program, no one killer innovation, no solitary lucky break, no miracle moment. Rather, the process resembles relentlessly pushing a giant, heavy flywheel in one direction, turn upon turn, building momentum until a point of breakthrough, and beyond.

STAGE 4: BUILDING GREATNESS TO LAST

Clock Building, Not Time Telling. Truly great organizations prosper through multiple generations of leaders, the exact opposite of being built around a single great leader, great idea or specific program. Leaders in great organizations build catalytic mechanisms to stimulate progress, and do not depend upon having a charismatic personality to get things done; indeed, many had a "charisma bypass."

Preserve the Core and Stimulate Progress. Enduring great organizations are characterized by a fundamental duality. On the one hand, they have a set of timeless core values and a core reason for being that remain constant over long periods of time. On the other hand, they have a relentless drive for change and progress—a creative compulsion that often manifests in BHAGs (Big Hairy Audacious Goals). Great organizations keep clear the difference between their core values (which never change) and operating strategies and cultural practices (which endlessly adapt to a changing world).

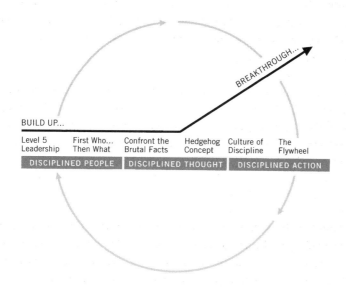

BUILD UP...

| Level 5 Leadership | First Who... Then What | Confront the Brutal Facts | Hedgehog Concept | Culture of Discipline | The Flywheel |

DISCIPLINED PEOPLE   DISCIPLINED THOUGHT   DISCIPLINED ACTION

*The principles in Stages 1-3 derive from the research for the book *Good to Great*, by Jim Collins; the principles in Stage 4 derive from the book *Built to Last*, by Jim Collins and Jerry I. Porras.

NOTES

1. Andrews, William J. and William J. Bratton, "What We've Learned About Policing," *City Journal*, Spring 1999.

2. Pooley, Eric, "One Good Apple," *Time*, January 15, 1996.

3. Tapellini, Donna, "Catalyst: William Bratton on Fighting Crime," *CIO Insight*, June 1, 2001.

4. These data are compiled by The U.S. Department of Education's Office of Postsecondary Education. The official title of the website is The OPE Equity in Athletics Disclosure Website; see http://ope.ed.gov/athletics.

5. Author interview with Tom Morris.

6. Helgesen, Sally, "The Pyramid and the Web," *New York Times*, May 27, 1990, F13.

7. Author interview with Frances Hesselbein, conducted when composing the foreword to *Hesselbein on Leadership*, (San Francisco: Jossey-Bass Publishers), 2002.

8. James MacGregor Burns, *Leadership*, (New York: Harper & Row, 1978), pp 9-28.

9. Author interview with Roger Briggs.

10. Author correspondence with Michael Brown.

11. Author correspondence with Wendy Kopp.

12. Author interview with John Morgan.

13. The Girl Scout Cookies® business operates at the level of Local Girl Scouts councils, and is not accounted for in the national organization form 990.

14. Author correspondence with Drew Buscareno.

15. According to the *Harvard University Gazette*, September 15, 2004, "Harvard University's endowment earned a 21.1% return during the year ending June 30, 2004, bringing the endowment's overall value to $22.6 billion."

16. Author correspondence with Tom Morris.

17. Birger, Jon, "30-Year Super Stocks," *Money Magazine*, October 9, 2002.

ABOUT THE AUTHOR

Photo by Ray Ng

Jim Collins has authored or co-authored five books, including *Built to Last, Good to Great* and *How the Mighty Fall*. Driven by a relentless curiosity, Jim began his research and teaching career on the faculty of Stanford's Graduate School of Business, where he received the Distinguished Teaching Award. In 1996, he returned to his hometown of Boulder, Colorado, to found his management laboratory, where he conducts research and works with leaders in the corporate and social sectors.

More about Jim and his works can be found at his e-teaching site, where he has assembled articles, audio clips, a recommended reading list, discussion guide, tools, and other information. The site is designed to be a place for students to study and learn. www.jimcollins.com